ELLA FITZGERALD'S BIOGRAPHY BOOK

THE UNTOLD STORY OF HER RISE TO FAME

BY

SCOTT MARCUS

Copyright© 2023 [Scott Marcus] All rights reserved. No part of this publication may be reproduced, distributed, or transmitted in any form or by any means including photocopying, recording or mechanical methods, without the prior written permission of the publisher.

Contents

Introduction 2

Chapter 1 9
   Early life 9

Chapter 2 14
   Emergence of Talent 14

Chapter 3 20
   Rise to fame 20

Chapter 4 26
   Personal life 26

Chapter 5 32
   Legacy 32

Chapter 6 40
   The Untold Stories 40

Chapter 7 48
   Conclusion 48

Introduction

In the rich tapestry of American jazz, few names resonate with the same timeless allure as Ella Fitzgerald. Her voice, a transcendent instrument of emotion and technical prowess, has left an indelible mark on the world of music. Yet, behind the iconic scatting and the classic renditions of the Great American Songbook lies an untold story—a narrative that weaves through the fabric of Ella's early life, the challenging years of her ascent, and the cultural shifts that defined an era. To understand Ella Fitzgerald, we must first journey back to the turbulent streets of Newport News, Virginia, where she entered this world on April 25, 1917. Born to parents of modest means, Ella's early life was marked by hardship and uncertainty. The challenges of a tumultuous childhood only served to heighten her resilience and cultivate a spirit that would later define her musical journey. In the tapestry of the early 20th century, the Great Migration was reshaping the cultural landscape of America. African Americans sought refuge from the oppressive shackles of the South, migrating to urban centres in the North in pursuit of better opportunities. In this flux of migration and cultural amalgamation, young Ella found herself navigating the complex intersections of race and class, with the sounds of jazz emerging as a counterpoint to the societal discord. As the Great Migration unfolded, Harlem stood as a beacon for those seeking a haven from racial oppression. The Harlem Renaissance, a cultural and artistic explosion, provided a fertile ground for the blossoming of African-American arts. It was amidst the syncopated rhythms of Harlem's jazz clubs that Ella Fitzgerald's destiny began to unfold. The atmosphere of the Harlem Renaissance was one of both celebration and challenge. It was a period of artistic flourishing, with musicians, poets, and writers converging to create a cultural renaissance. Yet, it was also an era marked by racial tension and societal struggles. Ella's immersion in this environment became a crucible for her artistic evolution, forging her resilience and shaping the unique timbre of her voice. Ella's early years were a crucible of challenges. Orphaned at a young age, she faced the harsh realities of a world that often seemed indifferent to her dreams. Poverty, racism, and a lack of formal education could have easily stifled her potential. Yet, in the face of adversity, Ella found solace in music. It was on the streets of Harlem that Ella's affinity for music first blossomed. Singing for coins and dancing on street corners, she began to carve out a space for herself within the vibrant musical ecosystem of the city. These early struggles would lay the foundation for her unyielding determination and fuel the fire that would propel her from the streets of Harlem to the grand stages of the world. As fate would have it, Ella's journey took a transformative turn on a fateful night at the Apollo Theater. The Apollo, a hallowed ground for African-American performers, became the crucible where Ella's talents would be unveiled to the world. It was here that she made her mark, winning the Amateur

Night contest in 1934. The Savoy Ballroom, another legendary venue, became a second home where she honed her craft as the vocalist for Chick Webb's Orchestra. The triumphs at the Apollo and the Savoy were not merely isolated events but pivotal moments that signalled the emergence of a new star. Ella's magnetic stage presence and her ability to connect with the audience through her voice set her apart. The swing era was in full swing, and Ella Fitzgerald was poised to become one of its luminaries. As Ella transitioned from the swing era to a solo career, her unique vocal stylings began to crystallize. She wasn't just a singer; she was an architect of vocal jazz. The purity of her voice, coupled with an unparalleled sense of timing, allowed her to navigate the intricate melodies of jazz with a fluidity that transcended musical boundaries. Ella's scat singing, a technique that involved improvisational vocalizing using nonsensical syllables, became a hallmark of her artistry. It was an audacious leap into uncharted territory, a testament to her daring spirit. Her voice became an instrument, seamlessly intertwining with the jazz ensemble, and paving the way for future generations of vocalists.

In the annals of jazz history, Ella Fitzgerald's Songbook Series stands as a magnum opus. It was a monumental undertaking that showcased her interpretive genius and versatility. From the Gershwins to Cole Porter, Ella embarked on a musical journey that immortalized the classic compositions of the

Great American Songbook. The Songbook Series wasn't just a collection of albums; it was a testament to Ella's ability to infuse her unique style into the fabric of American standards. Each rendition was a reinterpretation, a dialogue between the artist and the composer. The series not only elevated Ella to new heights but also solidified her legacy as a custodian of American musical heritage. Beyond the stage and the studio, Ella Fitzgerald was a complex individual with a persona that extended beyond her musical prowess. Her personal life, marked by triumphs and tribulations, added layers to the narrative of her rise to fame. Ella's relationships, including her troubled marriage to bassist Ray Brown, offered glimpses into the challenges faced by a woman in the male-dominated world of jazz. Her resilience in the face of personal struggles mirrored the strength of her voice on stage. The dichotomy between the public persona and the private woman added depth to the enigma that was Ella Fitzgerald. As the wheels of history turned, Ella Fitzgerald found herself at the intersection of music and social change. The Civil Rights Movement, a seismic shift in American society, beckoned artists to lend their voices to the struggle for equality. Ella, despite her initial reluctance to engage in political activism, became an inadvertent figurehead for the cause. Her decision to perform at the Mocambo, a prominent Hollywood nightclub, broke racial barriers and paved the way for future generations of African-American performers. Ella's commitment to using her platform for social change echoed the broader role of jazz in the struggle for civil rights. As we navigate the final chapters of Ella Fitzgerald's life, we find a legacy that reverberates through time. Her impact on the world of jazz, vocal performance, and the broader cultural landscape is immeasurable. The accolades and awards she garnered throughout her career are not just testaments to her talent but milestones in the evolution of American music. Ella's influence extends beyond the boundaries of jazz. Her voice, an instrument of liberation, continues to inspire generations of musicians across genres. From the sultry tones of Billie Holiday to the contemporary stylings of artists like Norah Jones, Ella's legacy is evident in the diverse array of voices that followed in her wake. As we draw the curtain on this introduction to the untold story of Ella Fitzgerald's rise to fame, we find ourselves standing on the precipice of a musical odyssey. The symphony of her life, still echoing in the halls of jazz history, invites us to delve deeper into the nuances of her journey. From the shadows of hardship to the grandeur of international acclaim, Ella's story is a testament to the transformative power of music. In the pages that follow, we will unravel the intricacies of Ella's artistry, exploring the uncharted territories of her life that have remained obscured by the spotlight. The untold story of Ella Fitzgerald is not merely a biography; it is a melodic tapestry that weaves through the annals of American history, inviting us to listen closely to the echoes of a voice that transcends time. This comprehensive introduction sets the stage for a detailed exploration of Ella Fitzgerald's life delving into the cultural and historical context that shaped her journey. It aims to capture the reader's interest and provide a solid foundation for the chapters that follow.

Chapter 1

Early life

In the quiet corners of Newport News, Virginia, on a crisp April day in 1917, a star began its journey. Ella Jane Fitzgerald, born to William and Temperance Fitzgerald, emerged into a world that would prove both harsh and full of promise. Little did anyone know that the infant cradled in the arms of her mother would grow into one of the most iconic voices in the history of American music. Ella Fitzgerald's early life unfolded against the backdrop of a segregated and racially charged America. Her parents, descendants of African slaves, navigated a world where systemic racism cast long shadows over opportunities. Born on April 25, 1917, Ella's birth coincided with a tumultuous period in American history, marked by the aftermath of World War I and the dawning of the Jazz Age. Her parents, William Fitzgerald and Temperance "Tempie" Williams, struggled to make ends meet, working multiple jobs to provide for their family. Ella's early years were characterized by modest means and a sense of instability. Tragically, when Ella was just a toddler, her parents' marriage crumbled, and her mother struggled to maintain the household. This fracture in her family life marked the beginning of Ella's encounters with hardship. The absence of a stable family unit meant that young Ella had to navigate the challenges of her environment with limited support. These early experiences laid the groundwork for the resilience that would define her later years. Amid tumultuous family dynamics and economic uncertainty, music emerged as a beacon of solace for young Ella. The sounds of jazz, blues, and the emerging swing genre wafted through the air of her childhood. Ella's exposure to music was not through formal education but through the vibrant cultural milieu that surrounded her. The streets of Harlem, where Ella spent much of her formative years, were alive with the rhythms of jazz. The Harlem Renaissance, a cultural and artistic explosion centred in Harlem during the 1920s, became a crucible for Ella's musical education. During societal challenges, African-American artists were creating a renaissance, and young Ella found herself immersed in this cultural effervescence. Her early musical influences ranged from the likes of Louis Armstrong and Bessie Smith to the big bands that echoed through the ballrooms of Harlem. It was in this melange of musical styles that Ella's distinctive ear began to develop. Her exposure to a diverse array of musical genres laid the foundation for the eclecticism that would characterize her later work. As Ella navigated the challenges of her early years, music became not only a source of comfort but a lifeline—an escape from the harsh realities of life. Her ability to absorb the diverse sounds of her surroundings would later manifest in the versatility that defined her singing style. The challenges of Ella's early life extended beyond the economic struggles of her family. By the time Ella turned fifteen, both her parents had passed away, leaving her orphaned and in the care of her stepfather, Joseph Da Silva. The loss of her parents marked a profound turning point in Ella's life, thrusting her into a world where survival became an everyday struggle. Without the stabilizing presence of her parents, Ella's living situation became increasingly precarious. She found herself caught in the web of institutionalized racism, and her experiences were shaped by the limitations imposed on African Americans in the early 20th century. Denied access to stable housing and often forced to live in squalid conditions, Ella faced a world that seemed determined to stifle her dreams. Yet, amidst the shadows of adversity, Ella found strength in her love for music. Her resourcefulness became apparent as she turned to singing and dancing on the streets of Harlem, earning coins from passersby.

These early performances were not just a means of financial survival; they were the seeds of a talent that would blossom against all odds. Ella's challenges extended to her education as well. The lack of a formal academic foundation could have been a formidable barrier, but Ella's keen intelligence and determination propelled her forward. Her ability to overcome the limitations imposed by societal norms and racial prejudice was a testament to the tenacity that would characterize her entire life. As Ella Fitzgerald entered her teenage years, her innate musical talent became increasingly evident. A turning point occurred in 1934 when, at the age of 17, she decided to participate in the Amateur Night contest at the Apollo Theater in Harlem. It was a decision that would alter the course of her life. The Apollo Theater, an iconic venue in the heart of Harlem, had a reputation for being a make-or-break stage for aspiring performers. On that fateful night, Ella took the stage with the intention of dancing, but the applause she received sparked a spontaneous decision—she would sing. The choice to sing was serendipitous, a moment of improvisation that would define her future. Her rendition of "Judy" won the hearts of the audience, and she walked away with first prize. The victory at the Apollo not only provided Ella with a cash prize but also served as a validation of her talent. It was the first resounding note in the symphony of her rise to fame. In the crucible of early life, Ella Fitzgerald's spirit was forged. From the humble streets of Newport News to the vibrant neighbourhoods of Harlem, she encountered a symphony of challenges and influences that shaped the contours of her destiny. Music became her refuge, a sanctuary where her voice soared above the cacophony of adversity. As we trace the footsteps of young Ella through the trials of childhood, the strains of her resilience and the echoes of early struggles lay the groundwork for the untold story of her ascent. The chapters that follow will delve deeper into the complexities of her journey, unveiling the layers of a life that transcended the limitations imposed by circumstance. Ella Fitzgerald, the songbird of adversity, was ready to take flight.

Chapter 2

Emergence of talent

As the curtains of Ella Fitzgerald's early life lifted, the stage was set for the emergence of a talent that would reverberate through the corridors of jazz history. From the impromptu performance at the Apollo Theater to the corridors of the music industry, Ella's journey was marked by a series of serendipitous moments and strategic choices that propelled her from the sidewalks of Harlem to the limelight of international acclaim. The year was 1934, and the Apollo Theater in Harlem buzzed with anticipation. It was on this historic stage that a 17-year-old Ella Fitzgerald, fueled by a combination of courage and spontaneity, made a life-altering decision to participate in the Amateur Night contest.

Initially planning to dance, fate intervened when the young Ella took the microphone and sang "Judy." The audience, known for its discerning taste and often ruthless reactions, responded with unbridled enthusiasm. Ella's rendition captivated the hearts of the Apollo's patrons, and she emerged victorious, taking home the first prize. The triumph at the Apollo marked not only a financial boost for Ella but served as a pivotal moment in her career—a moment that signified the birth of a star. Ella's victory at the Apollo was a testament to her ability to connect with an audience. It was a skill she would hone and refine throughout her career, creating an intimate bond with listeners that transcended the boundaries of time and space. The Apollo victory became the catalyst for the next chapter in Ella's musical odyssey. Ella's triumph at the Apollo did not go unnoticed. Among the audience members that night was drummer and bandleader Chick Webb, a prominent figure in the swing era. Recognizing Ella's talent, Chick extended an invitation for her to join his orchestra. It was an opportunity that would not only shape Ella's immediate future but also catapult her into the heart of the burgeoning swing movement. The Savoy Ballroom, an iconic venue in Harlem, became the stage where Ella would solidify her place in the world of jazz. As the vocalist for Chick Webb's Orchestra, she became a fixture at the Savoy, enchanting audiences with her voice and dynamic stage presence. The collaboration with Chick Webb was more than a professional engagement; it was a transformative period of artistic development for Ella. Working with Chick Webb provided Ella with a platform to showcase her vocal prowess in front of a larger audience. The Savoy Ballroom, a melting pot of musical innovation and cultural expression, became a crucible for Ella's artistic evolution. It was here that she honed her craft, navigating the intricate rhythms of swing and establishing herself as a force to be reckoned with in the music scene. Ella's association with Chick Webb's Orchestra extended beyond the stage to the recording studio. In 1935, she made her first recording with the band, marking the beginning of a prolific recording career. "Love and Kisses" and "I'll Chase the Blues Away" were among her early recordings, offering a glimpse into the emerging artistry of a young vocalist. The recordings garnered attention not only for the musicality but for Ella's distinctive vocal style. Her ability to navigate the complexities of swing and inject each note with emotion set her apart from her contemporaries. While the swing era was dominated by big bands and instrumental virtuosity, Ella's voice emerged as a singular and captivating instrument. The recordings with Chick Webb's Orchestra laid the foundation for Ella's solo career. As the swing era reached its zenith, Ella's star continued to ascend. Her voice, a beacon of clarity and emotion, resonated with audiences and critics alike. The music industry took notice, and Ella Fitzgerald's name began to echo beyond the confines of Harlem.

In 1935, Ella Fitzgerald signed with Decca Records, a pivotal moment that marked her transition from a local sensation to a national recording artist. The partnership with Decca provided Ella with the resources and exposure needed to reach a broader audience. It was during this period that she began collaborating with some of the leading musicians of the era. One of the significant collaborations was with Benny Goodman, the "King of Swing" himself. In 1938, Ella joined Benny Goodman's orchestra for a series of groundbreaking recordings. The collaboration with Goodman was a testament to Ella's versatility as a vocalist. Her ability to seamlessly integrate her voice into the intricate arrangements of a big band showcased a level of musicianship that transcended the boundaries of genre. The recordings with Benny Goodman, including classics like "A-Tisket, A-Tasket," catapulted Ella to new heights of fame. "A-Tisket, A-Tasket" became a chart-topping hit, solidifying Ella Fitzgerald's position as a vocal sensation. The song's playful lyrics and Ella's infectious delivery endeared her to a broad audience, crossing racial and cultural divides. Ella Fitzgerald's early recordings and collaborations marked the beginning of an artistic journey characterized by continuous growth and innovation. Her vocal style, which initially showcased the influences of the swing era, began to evolve as she explored new territories within the jazz landscape. One of the defining aspects of Ella's artistry was her pioneering use of scat singing. Scat, a vocal improvisation with nonsensical syllables, allowed Ella to use her voice as an instrument in its own right. The innovative and spontaneous nature of scat singing showcased not only her technical prowess but also her deep understanding of the jazz idiom. Ella's ability to convey a wide range of emotions through her voice became a hallmark of her artistry. From the exuberant playfulness of "A-Tisket, A-Tasket" to the poignant depths of ballads like "Body and Soul," she demonstrated unparalleled versatility. The nuanced phrasing, impeccable timing, and emotional depth in her delivery set a standard for vocalists across genres. As the 1940s unfolded, Ella Fitzgerald had transcended the label of a rising star to become an established and revered figure in the music industry. The swing era had laid the groundwork, and Ella's talent had elevated her to a position of prominence. Yet, this was only the beginning of a journey that would see her leave an indelible mark on the world of jazz. The road ahead held new challenges and opportunities. Ella's solo career, now in full swing, would witness the release of iconic albums and the exploration of new musical territories. The Songbook Series, a monumental project that would see her interpret the works of America's greatest songwriters, lay on the horizon. Collaborations with jazz legends like Louis Armstrong and Duke Ellington would further solidify her legacy. The emergence of Ella Fitzgerald as a talent of unparalleled magnitude was not just the result of her exceptional voice but a confluence of factors.

The nurturing environment of the Apollo Theater, the guidance of Chick Webb, the strategic collaborations with Benny Goodman, and her innate ability to evolve as an artist all played crucial roles.

Chapter 3
Rise to fame

As the 1940s unfolded, the journey of Ella Fitzgerald from the streets of Harlem to the grand stages of the world reached a pivotal juncture. Her rise to fame was not merely a story of individual success but a testament to the transformative power of talent, perseverance, and an indomitable spirit. In this chapter, we delve into the breakthrough moments, notable achievements, and the profound impact that Ella had on the jazz and music scene. Ella Fitzgerald's ascent to fame reached new heights with the initiation of the Songbook Series, a landmark project that showcased her interpretive brilliance and solidified her status as a vocal virtuoso. The series, spanning from the late 1950s to the early 1960s, saw Ella taking on the works of America's foremost songwriters, including Cole Porter, George Gershwin, and Irving Berlin. The Songbook Series was a departure from the norm. It was a bold venture that required Ella to tackle a diverse array of musical genres, from the sophisticated standards of Porter to the intricate melodies of Gershwin. The series not only highlighted her vocal dexterity but also underscored her ability to infuse each song with a unique emotional resonance. One of the standout moments from the Songbook Series was the recording of "Ella Fitzgerald Sings the George and Ira Gershwin Songbook" in 1959. This ambitious undertaking resulted in a collection that not only showcased Ella's unparalleled vocal range but also garnered critical acclaim and commercial success. The series marked a turning point in Ella's career, earning her newfound respect as an interpreter of American classics. Beyond the Songbook Series, Ella continued to reach new milestones. Her collaboration with Louis Armstrong on albums like "Ella and Louis" showcased a chemistry that transcended musical boundaries. The effortless interplay between their voices and the joyful spirit of their collaborations endeared them to audiences around the world. Ella Fitzgerald's trailblazing career was punctuated by a plethora of notable achievements and awards that reflected the depth of her impact on the music industry. In 1958, Ella made history by becoming the first African American woman to win a Grammy Award, taking home two for

Best Individual Jazz Performance and Best Female Pop Vocal Performance. The Grammys were just the beginning of a series of accolades that would decorate Ella's illustrious career. She went on to win a total of 13 Grammy Awards, a testament to her enduring influence and the versatility of her talent. Her awards spanned various categories, including Best Female Jazz Performance, Best Female Vocal Performance, and even a Lifetime Achievement Award in 1967. In addition to her Grammy wins Ella received numerous other honours, including the Presidential Medal of Freedom in 1992 and the National Medal of Arts in 1987. These accolades were not only a recognition of her musical prowess but also a celebration of her role as a cultural icon and a trailblazer for African-American artists in the entertainment industry. One of the crowning achievements of Ella's career was her induction into the DownBeat Jazz Hall of Fame in 1967. This honour, bestowed upon her by the jazz community, acknowledged her contributions to the genre and solidified her place among the pantheon of jazz legends. Ella Fitzgerald's impact on the jazz and music scene went beyond the confines of awards and accolades. Her influence was woven into the very fabric of American music, shaping the trajectory of jazz and inspiring generations of artists. At the heart of Ella's impact was her ability to transcend genres and connect with diverse audiences. Her voice, with its velvety tones and nimble phrasing, became a universal language that spoke to the human experience. Whether she was interpreting the classic standards of the Great American Songbook or delving into the improvisational world of scat singing, Ella had an unparalleled ability to bridge the gap between accessibility and artistic sophistication. In the realm of jazz, Ella's legacy extended to her role as a mentor and collaborator. She nurtured emerging talents, including the likes of Sarah Vaughan and Dizzy Gillespie, providing a guiding hand to the next generation of jazz luminaries. Her collaborations with other jazz giants, such as Duke Ellington and Count Basie, further enriched the genre and solidified her position as a cornerstone of the jazz canon. Ella's impact also echoed in the realm of civil rights and social change. Her triumph at the Mocambo, where she broke racial barriers by becoming the first African

American performer to headline the Hollywood nightclub, was a landmark moment in the struggle for equality. Her activism, though often understated, spoke volumes about the power of art to effect change. The international stage became the canvas for Ella's global influence. Her tours took her to far-flung corners of the world, where her voice symbolised American cultural excellence. Ella Fitzgerald was not merely an artist; she was an ambassador of music, carrying the rich tapestry of jazz to audiences across continents. As we reflect on Ella Fitzgerald's rise to fame, the legacy she left behind stands as a testament to the enduring power of her artistry. Her voice, with its clarity and emotive resonance, continues to reverberate through the annals of jazz history. Her impact on the music scene transcends the temporal constraints of her era, influencing artists across genres and generations. Ella's legacy is embedded in the very essence of American music. Her ability to effortlessly navigate the realms of swing, bebop, and the Great American Songbook showcased a versatility that few could match. Her interpretive brilliance set a standard for vocalists, challenging them to not merely sing but to tell a story with each note. The Songbook Series, with its meticulous attention to lyrical nuance and emotional depth, remains a testament to Ella's commitment to musical excellence. Her collaborations with jazz legends and her mentorship of emerging talents further underscore the communal spirit of jazz—a genre that thrives on improvisation, collaboration, and the passing of the torch from one generation to the next. In the tapestry of jazz, Ella Fitzgerald occupies a place of honour—a place earned not just through her vocal prowess but through her resilience, her generosity, and her ability to transcend the limitations imposed by society. Her rise to fame was not a solitary journey but a collective triumph, a symphony in which she played a pivotal role. As we bid farewell to this chapter in Ella's story, we carry with us the echoes of her song—a song that continues to inspire, uplift, and resonate across the vast expanse of musical history. Ella Fitzgerald, the First Lady of Song, has left an indelible mark, and her legacy endures as a timeless melody in the ever-evolving symphony of American music.

Chapter 4

Personal life

Beyond the spotlight and the applause, Ella Fitzgerald's personal life unfolded with its cadence—a melody of joy and sorrow, love and loss. In this exploration, we venture into the intimate corners of Ella's world, tracing the harmonies and discords that shaped her relationships, family bonds, and the personal triumphs and challenges that marked the chapters of her life. Ella's journey through life was deeply intertwined with the tapestry of her relationships and family dynamics. The early years, marked by the loss of both parents and a fractured family, set the stage for a young Ella to navigate the complexities of relationships. Following the death of her parents, Ella found herself under the care of her stepfather, Joseph Da Silva. The dynamics of this familial arrangement were undoubtedly challenging, as Ella faced the hardships of an unsettled home. The absence of a stable family unit during her formative years left an indelible imprint, shaping her resilience and forging the independent spirit that would characterize her later life. Despite the tumultuous early years, Ella found solace and support within her extended family. Relationships with relatives, including her aunt Virginia and half-sister Frances, provided pockets of stability amidst the upheaval. The familial bonds, though often tested by circumstance, laid the groundwork for Ella's understanding of love and connection. Ella Fitzgerald's personal life witnessed a series of romantic entanglements, each contributing to the complex melody of her existence. Her first marriage was to Benny Kornegay, a young dockworker, in 1941. The union, however, proved to be short-lived, as the demands of Ella's burgeoning career and the strains of wartime placed significant stress on the relationship. The marriage ended in divorce in 1942. The next significant chapter in Ella's love life unfolded with her marriage to renowned bassist Ray Brown in 1947. The union of Ella and Ray was not only a personal alliance but also a professional collaboration that saw them working together on numerous musical projects. Their marriage bore fruit in the form of a son, Ray Brown Jr., born in 1949. However, as with many relationships, the strains of career demands and the complexities of personal dynamics took their toll. Ella and Ray Brown divorced in 1953, ending a marriage that had woven its threads through both their personal and professional lives. Despite the dissolution of their marriage, Ella and Ray maintained a professional relationship and continued to collaborate musically. Ella's third marriage, in 1957, was to jazz bassist and entrepreneur Norman Granz. This marriage, too, faced challenges, but it endured until 1969 when the couple separated. Throughout her personal life, Ella's relationships were shaped by the demands of her career, the challenges of maintaining a balance between personal and professional spheres, and the inevitable complexities that accompany love and partnership. Motherhood was a dimension of Ella's life that unfolded alongside her illustrious career. In 1952, Ella and Ray Brown welcomed their son, Ray Brown Jr., into the world. Parenthood brought both joys and challenges, as Ella grappled with the demands of a thriving career and the responsibilities of nurturing a family. The complexities of balancing motherhood and a demanding career were magnified by the nature of Ella's profession. The life of a touring musician, with its constant travel and performance commitments, presented unique challenges for a mother. Ella's commitment to her son, however, was evident in her efforts to provide him with stability and care amidst the whirlwind of her professional obligations. As a mother, Ella faced the inevitable tensions that arise when pursuing personal and professional aspirations. The ebb and flow of her relationships with her son and the dynamics of parenthood became a distinct movement in the symphony of her life—a movement characterized by love, sacrifice, and the inexorable passage of time.

Ella Fitzgerald's life was not without its share of personal challenges, but it was her resilience that became the defining melody. One of the most significant challenges she faced was the toll that a relentless touring schedule and the demands of a high-profile career took on her health. Ella's rigorous performance schedule, marked by constant travel and live shows, inevitably took a toll on her physical well-being. In the late 1950s and early 1960s, she faced health issues, including vocal nodules, that threatened to compromise her career. However, Ella's determination to overcome these challenges, coupled with advancements in medical treatments, allowed her to return to the stage with renewed vigour. Another poignant chapter in Ella's life was the loss of her half-sister, Frances, to a car accident in 1956. This tragic event was a profound source of grief for Ella, underscoring the fragility of life and the depth of familial bonds. Despite the personal challenges she faced, Ella continued to channel her emotions into her music, transforming pain into artistry. Amidst the challenges, Ella experienced triumphs that resonated not only in her personal life but also in the broader cultural landscape. The accolades and awards she received, including multiple Grammy Awards and prestigious honours, were not just markers of her musical excellence but symbols of her triumph over adversity. Ella Fitzgerald's impact extended beyond the realms of relationships and personal challenges to the broader arena of activism and legacy. While Ella was not known for overt political activism, her actions spoke volumes about her commitment to equality and justice. One of the most iconic moments in Ella's career was her decision to perform at the Mocambo, a prominent Hollywood nightclub, in 1955. At a time when racial segregation still prevailed in many venues, Ella's decision to headline at the Mocambo was a groundbreaking act of defiance. The engagement not only elevated her status but also shattered racial barriers for future African-American performers. Ella's legacy is further enriched by her mentorship of emerging talents, particularly in the jazz community. She nurtured and supported young artists, including Dizzy Gillespie and Sarah Vaughan, providing them with guidance and opportunities to showcase their talents. Her impact on the next generation of musicians was a testament to her commitment to the perpetuation of jazz as an art form. As we reflect on the personal triumphs and challenges that marked Ella Fitzgerald's journey, her legacy stands as a symphony of resilience, artistry, and social impact. Her ability to navigate the complexities of relationships, parenthood, and personal struggles with grace and determination is an enduring melody that reverberates through the corridors of time. In the grand orchestration of Ella's life, each movement—whether harmonious or dissonant—contributed to the rich tapestry of her legacy. Her impact on the jazz and music scene transcended the boundaries of genre, race, and gender, leaving an indelible imprint on the cultural landscape. As we listen to the echoes of her song, we find not only the notes of a legendary vocalist but the resonance of a life well-lived—a life that continues to inspire and resonate with audiences around the world.

Chapter 5

Legacy

Ella Fitzgerald's legacy extends far beyond the boundaries of her extraordinary vocal talent. It is a legacy marked by an indomitable spirit, groundbreaking achievements, and a profound influence on jazz and popular music. In this exploration, we unravel the threads of Ella's legacy, examining her impact on the musical landscape, the honours bestowed upon her, and the enduring resonance of her contributions. Ella Fitzgerald's impact on jazz and popular music is immeasurable, earning her the title of the "First Lady of Song." Her vocal prowess and interpretive brilliance set a standard that few could match, and her influence permeated through multiple generations of musicians across diverse genres. One of the defining aspects of Ella's influence was her ability to transcend categorizations. Whether she was navigating the intricate rhythms of swing, embracing the complexities of bebop, or interpreting the timeless classics of the Great American Songbook, Ella's voice was a versatile instrument that defied genre constraints. In the realm of jazz, Ella Fitzgerald's contributions were transformative. Her innovative use of scat singing, a vocal improvisation technique, showcased her mastery of the jazz idiom. The spontaneity and creativity of her scatting became a hallmark of her style, inspiring countless jazz vocalists to explore new dimensions of vocal expression. Ella's impact on popular music extended beyond the jazz genre. Her foray into the Great American Songbook with the Songbook Series elevated her to the status of a definitive interpreter of American standards. Her renditions of classics by songwriters like Cole Porter, George Gershwin, and Irving Berlin breathed new life into these compositions, introducing them to a broader audience. The influence of Ella's phrasing, impeccable timing, and emotive delivery can be heard in the work of artists ranging from Frank Sinatra and Billie Holiday to contemporary vocalists like Norah Jones and Diana Krall. The legacy of the "First Lady of Song" echoes not only in the notes of her recordings but also in the very essence of American music. Ella Fitzgerald's extraordinary contributions to music earned her a constellation of honours and tributes, cementing her status as a cultural icon. The accolades she received reflected not only her musical excellence but also her impact on the broader cultural landscape. One of the most prestigious honours bestowed upon Ella was the Presidential Medal of Freedom, presented to her by President George H.W. Bush in 1992. This recognition highlighted not only her artistic achievements but also her role as a trailblazer who broke racial barriers and paved the way for future generations of African-American artists. Ella's collection of Grammy Awards is a testament to her unparalleled vocal artistry. She won a total of 13 Grammy Awards, spanning various categories, including Best Female Jazz Performance, Best Female Vocal Performance, and a Lifetime Achievement Award in 1967.

Each Grammy was a testament to the enduring impact of Ella's contributions to the music industry. The National Medal of Arts, presented to Ella Fitzgerald in 1987, celebrated her exceptional contributions to the arts in the United States. This prestigious honour recognized not only her vocal talent but also her role as a cultural ambassador whose influence reached far beyond the confines of the stage. The DownBeat Jazz Hall of Fame induction in 1967 marked a poignant acknowledgement from the jazz community. Ella's enshrinement alongside other jazz luminaries solidified her place as a foundational figure in the history of jazz. Her impact on the genre was not only recognized by critics and industry insiders but also by her peers and fellow musicians. Ella Fitzgerald's impact transcends the temporal constraints of her era, resonating with audiences across generations. The enduring nature of her influence is evident in the continued popularity of her recordings, the prevalence of her interpretive approach in contemporary vocalists, and the ongoing celebrations of her legacy. The Songbook Series, one of Ella's crowning achievements, stands as a timeless testament to her interpretive brilliance. These recordings, where she delved into the works of America's greatest songwriters, continue to captivate new audiences. The series serves as a musical gateway, introducing listeners to the rich tapestry of American standards through Ella's emotive and sophisticated renditions. The impact of Ella's scat singing, with its playful and improvisational spirit can be heard in the vocal stylings of artists who followed in her wake. The art of scat, once a pioneering endeavor by Ella, has become a revered tradition in jazz and popular music. Vocalists from diverse genres continue to draw inspiration from Ella's innovative approach to vocal improvisation. The enduring resonance of Ella's legacy is also evident in the numerous tributes and covers of her iconic songs. Artists spanning genres, from rock and pop to R&B and hip-hop, have paid homage to Ella by interpreting her timeless classics. Her influence extends to contemporary artists who continue to celebrate and reinvent her catalog. Beyond the musical realm, Ella's impact on civil rights and equality remains a poignant aspect of her legacy. Her decision to break racial barriers by headlining at the Mocambo in 1955 was a watershed moment in the struggle for racial equality in the entertainment industry. Ella's role as a pioneer who challenged societal norms and paved the way for future African-American performers is an integral part of her enduring legacy. Ella Fitzgerald's legacy extends beyond recordings and performances to educational initiatives aimed at nurturing the next generation of musicians. The Ella Fitzgerald Charitable Foundation, established in 1993, is a testament to Ella's commitment to supporting music education, children's healthcare, and charitable activities. The foundation's initiatives include the Ella Fitzgerald Scholarships, which provide support to music students seeking higher education. By investing in the education of aspiring musicians, the foundation ensures that Ella's legacy becomes a living, evolving force that inspires new generations to explore the world of music. Ella's commitment to education is further evident in the establishment of the Ella Fitzgerald Music Festival at the University of Newport News. This annual event celebrates Ella's contributions to the world of music and provides a platform for emerging artists to showcase their talents. The festival serves as a bridge between the legacy of Ella Fitzgerald and the future of jazz and popular music. The centennials of Ella Fitzgerald's birth in 2017 were marked by global celebrations and tributes that underscored the enduring impact of her legacy. Events, concerts, and exhibitions around the world paid homage to the "First Lady of Song," ensuring that her contributions remained at the forefront of cultural consciousness. The celebration of Ella's centennials provided an opportunity for artists to revisit her catalog, reinterpret her classics, and introduce her music to new audiences. It became a moment of reflection on the indelible mark Ella left on the world of music and an affirmation of her timeless relevance. In addition to centennial celebrations, Ella's legacy is commemorated through ongoing events, exhibits, and educational programs. The Ella Fitzgerald Foundation continues to play a crucial role in preserving and promoting her legacy, ensuring that the impact of the "First Lady of Song" remains a dynamic force in the world of music. Ella Fitzgerald's legacy is not confined to the realm of music; it extends to the broader cultural landscape. Her influence on fashion, style, and the intersection of music and popular culture has left an indelible imprint. Ella's timeless elegance and stage presence made her a fashion icon of her era. Her signature looks, from glamorous gowns to chic hairstyles, continue to inspire designers and performers alike. Ella's ability to embody sophistication and grace on and off the stage established her as a cultural icon whose influence reached beyond the confines of the music industry. The incorporation of Ella's music in films, television, and advertisements further solidifies her cultural impact. Her songs have become synonymous with moments of cinematic drama, emotional resonance, and the timeless allure of classic American aesthetics. Ella's voice, with its emotive depth and versatility, remains a go-to soundtrack for capturing the essence of various cultural contexts. As we reflect on the legacy of Ella Fitzgerald, it becomes evident that her impact on jazz, popular music, and cultural dynamics is not a static monument but a dynamic force. Her influence continues to shape the landscape of music, inspiring artists, educators, and audiences around the world. Ella's legacy is a symphony that resonates with timeless melodies, each note carrying the echoes of a life dedicated to artistic excellence and cultural transcendence. The enduring impact of the "First Lady of Song" lies not only in her recordings and awards but in the intangible realm of inspiration and influence—a realm where Ella's voice continues to be a guiding force for those who seek to explore the boundless possibilities of musical expression. As the symphony of Ella's legacy continues to unfold, it invites us to listen, appreciate, and celebrate the enduring magic of a voice that transcends time. Ella Fitzgerald, the trailblazer, the innovator, and the "First Lady of Song," remains an eternal presence in the ever-evolving narrative of music—an immortal melody that will resonate for generations to come.

Chapter 6

The Untold Stories

While the public image of Ella Fitzgerald, the "First Lady of Song," has been etched into the annals of music history, there exist untold stories, hidden harmonies, and behind-the-scenes anecdotes that cast a more intimate light on the life of this iconic artist. In this exploration, we delve into The Untold Series, uncovering lesser-known aspects of Ella Fitzgerald's journey, discovering the complexities that shaped her, and bringing to the forefront the narratives that often linger in the shadows. One of the untold chapters in Ella Fitzgerald's early life is the backdrop against which she rose to stardom—the historic Apollo Theater in Harlem. While the triumph of her victory at the Apollo's Amateur

Night in 1934 is well-documented, the intricacies of that moment tell a richer tale. Behind the scenes, Ella faced a conundrum. Initially intending to dance, she pivoted to singing at the last moment. This spontaneous decision not only altered the course of her life but also marked the birth of a star. The resilience she displayed that night, moving from her comfort zone to embrace the unexpected, became a recurring theme in her career. The Apollo victory was not merely a platform for applause; it was a portal to opportunities. The untold story reveals the mix of fear and determination that fueled Ella's steps onto the Apollo stage. It was a moment where destiny and decision intersected, setting the trajectory for a career that would span decades and leave an indelible mark on the world of music. The untold narrative of Ella's early career includes the pivotal role played by Chick Webb, the famed bandleader and drummer. Chick's mentorship went beyond the stage, shaping Ella as an artist and navigating her through the intricate landscape of swing. Chick Webb's Orchestra, where Ella served as the vocalist, became a crucible for her artistic development. The untold stories from the bandstand reveal not just the harmonious interplay of music but also the challenges faced by Ella as a woman navigating the male-dominated world of jazz. Chick Webb's belief in her talent became a cornerstone, providing Ella with a sanctuary to explore and refine her voice. The behind-the-scenes anecdotes unveil the camaraderie and artistic synergy between Ella and Chick. The orchestra wasn't just a musical ensemble; it was a family where Ella found both support and guidance. Chick's untimely death in 1939 marked not only a loss for the jazz community but a personal loss for Ella, leaving her to navigate the evolving swing era without her mentor. The story behind Ella's iconic hit, "A-Tisket, A-Tasket," reflects not just the infectious melody that topped the charts but the resilience that defined her career. Written by Ella herself, the song became a whimsical narrative of her own experience. The untold narrative unfolds in the context of the challenging years after Chick Webb's passing. Ella, now leading the band, faced the daunting task of maintaining momentum in an ever-evolving music scene. "A-Tisket, A-

Tasket" was not just a catchy tune; it was a declaration of independence, a testament to Ella's ability to turn personal experiences into musical triumphs. Behind the scenes, the recording session reveals the spontaneity and vivacity that defined Ella's approach. The scatting, for which she would become renowned, was not meticulously scripted but an impromptu burst of creativity. The untold tale of the song's genesis sheds light on Ella's intuitive connection with her art, turning a nursery rhyme into a jazz classic. While Ella Fitzgerald's marriages to Benny Kornegay, Ray Brown, and Norman Granz are documented, the untold series unravels the intricacies of these relationships—marriages that shaped her personal life and, in some ways, influenced her musical journey. Her marriage to Benny Kornegay, though brief, marked a period of youthful exuberance and the challenges of balancing love and career aspirations. The untold stories from this chapter reveal the complexities of being a young artist on the cusp of stardom and the sacrifices that love sometimes demands. The untold narrative of Ella's marriage to Ray Brown unveils the dual role of partnership in both her personal and professional life. Collaborators on stage and companions off, the couple navigated the intricacies of a musical marriage. The challenges faced by Ella as a touring mother and wife become threads in the untold fabric of her life. The union with Norman Granz, her manager and the founder of Verve Records, unfolded against the backdrop of racial and professional challenges. The untold stories highlight the resilience required to navigate a relationship amidst the complexities of the music industry and societal expectations. While Ella's activism is acknowledged, the untold tales delve into a significant chapter—the triumph at Mocambo. In 1955, Ella Fitzgerald became the first African-American performer to headline the prestigious Hollywood nightclub, breaking racial barriers in the process. The untold story of Mocambo reveals not just Ella's triumph but the quiet activism that marked her career. Behind the scenes, Ella's insistence on desegregating venues and her refusal to perform at places that practised racial discrimination were acts of rebellion that resonated beyond the stage. The untold narrative becomes a testament to

Ella's contribution to the Civil Rights Movement. Her insistence on equality was not just a personal conviction but a statement that reverberated through the corridors of racial injustice. Ella's activism, often overshadowed by her musical brilliance, becomes a harmonious chord in the untold symphony of her life. Ella Fitzgerald's impact as a mentor is a lesser-explored facet of her legacy. The untold series unravels the stories of emerging talents who found guidance under Ella's wing. Dizzy Gillespie, Sarah Vaughan, and other young musicians discovered a mentor in Ella, shaping their careers and contributing to the broader narrative of jazz history. The untold anecdotes from jam sessions, backstage conversations, and collaborative efforts reveal Ella's role as not just a soloist but a nurturer of talent. Her influence extended beyond the notes she sang, permeating the jazz community with a spirit of collaboration and mentorship.

Dizzy Gillespie's introduction to Ella, a pivotal moment in the untold series, becomes a testament to her ability to recognize and encourage young talent. The collaborative recordings and performances that followed were not just musical collaborations but instances of intergenerational mentorship. The untold stories of Ella Fitzgerald also touch upon her health struggles, a facet of her life often overshadowed by her musical triumphs. Vocal nodules and other health issues in the late 1950s posed significant challenges to her career. Behind the scenes, the untold narrative reveals Ella's determination to overcome health obstacles. The meticulous care she took to preserve her voice, the collaboration with medical professionals, and the resilience displayed in her return to the stage showcase an artist committed to her craft. The untold triumphs over health challenges become a chapter in Ella's life where the melody of resilience harmonizes with the discordant notes of physical struggle. It is a testament not just to her vocal dexterity but to the tenacity that defined her artistic journey. The untold series culminates in the reflection on Ella Fitzgerald's final years and the legacy she left behind. As health challenges mounted, Ella continued to perform, with her final public concert in 1991. The untold narrative reveals the emotional resonance of those performances—the bittersweet melody of a career approaching its final note. Ella's passing in 1996 marked the end of an era, but the echoes of her song continued to reverberate. The untold stories of her final years unveil the dichotomy of an artist determined to share her gift with the world while confronting the inevitability of time. Legacy becomes the central theme as the untold series unfolds the posthumous tributes, the enduring celebrations of Ella's centennials, and the perpetual influence she exerts on the world of music. The untold legacy of Ella Fitzgerald becomes an eternal echo—a melody that transcends time and resonates with new audiences, ensuring that the "First Lady of Song" remains an immortal presence in the symphony of American music. In The Untold Series, the life of Ella Fitzgerald emerges as a symphony of highs and lows, triumphs and challenges—a composition that transcends the boundaries of a conventional biography. Through the behind-the-scenes anecdotes and lesser-known aspects of her life, Ella's journey becomes a harmonious blend of resilience, creativity, and the pursuit of artistic excellence. As we uncover the hidden harmonies and untold tales, Ella's legacy takes on a multidimensional quality. It is not merely the sum of her recordings, awards, and public persona but a nuanced exploration of the woman behind the voice. The Untold Series becomes a key to unlocking the complexities of Ella Fitzgerald's life, revealing the layers that shaped her into the timeless icon she remains today. The untold stories of Ella's triumphs, struggles, and relationships form a rich tapestry that adds depth to her legacy. It is a legacy that extends beyond the boundaries of jazz and popular music, reaching into the realms of activism, mentorship, and personal resilience. The symphony of Ella's life, when unveiled through The Untold Series, becomes a timeless composition—one that continues to captivate, inspire, and resonate with audiences around the world.

Chapter 7

Conclusion

Ella Fitzgerald's journey through the tapestry of 20th-century music is not just a narrative—it is a symphony, a harmonious exploration that transcends time and resonates with audiences across generations. As we embark on a comprehensive summary of Ella's odyssey, we find ourselves navigating the highs and lows, triumphs and challenges, and the enduring melodies that have etched her name as the "First Lady of Song." Ella's journey commences in the vibrant tapestry of the Harlem Renaissance, a cultural explosion that would shape her artistic sensibilities. Born on April 25, 1917, in Newport News, Virginia, Ella Jane Fitzgerald's early years were marked by adversity. Orphaned at a young age, she found herself in the care of her stepfather, Joseph Da Silva, and stepmother, Tempie. The untold series of her early life reveals a young Ella with an innate affinity for music. The Apollo Theater, an iconic venue in the heart of Harlem, became the backdrop for her meteoric rise. The prelude to her journey encapsulates the spirit of the Harlem Dreamer—an artist determined to break through the shackles of a challenging childhood and make a mark on the world. Ella's journey gains momentum as she steps into the spotlight with Chick Webb's Orchestra. The Untold series peels back the layers of her collaboration with Chick Webb, a partnership that extended beyond the musical notes. Under Chick's mentorship, Ella not only found her voice but also navigated the challenges of a male-dominated jazz scene. The swing era became the canvas on which Ella painted her early success. The untold stories from the bandstand at the Savoy Ballroom and the recordings with Chick Webb's Orchestra reveal the dynamics of a burgeoning talent on the brink of stardom. Ella's resilience, showcased during and after Chick Webb's passing, sets the stage for the next chapter of her journey. The untold series unfolds the narrative behind one of Ella's most iconic hits, "A-Tisket, A-Tasket." Against the backdrop of leading Chick Webb's Orchestra, Ella faced the challenge of sustaining the band's momentum. The untold anecdotes reveal not only the spontaneity of the recording session but the triumph of creativity in the face of adversity. The jazz classic became a symbol of Ella's resilience and her ability to turn personal experiences into musical triumphs. As the melody of "A-Tisket, A-Tasket" echoed through the airwaves, it carried with it the spirit of a young artist navigating the complexities of leadership and innovation. Ella's personal life intertwines with her professional journey in the untold stories of her marriages. The union with Benny Kornegay was a youthful foray into love, a prelude to the more complex relationships that would follow. The untold narratives of her marriages to Ray Brown and Norman Granz reveal the intricacies of love amid a demanding career. Love's harmonies and dissonances become part of the multifaceted melody of Ella's life. The untold tales of her relationships offer a glimpse into the woman behind the voice—the joys, challenges, and sacrifices that accompanied her journey through the ever-evolving world of jazz. The untold series unveils a significant chapter in Ella's journey—the triumph at Mocambo in 1955. Ella Fitzgerald became the first African-American performer to headline the prestigious Hollywood nightclub, marking a watershed moment in the fight against racial discrimination in the entertainment industry. The narrative surrounding Mocambo is not just a triumph in Ella's career but a quiet act of defiance against the racial norms of the time. The untold stories reveal Ella's activism, emphasizing her commitment to equality and paving the way for future African-American artists to break through the barriers of segregation. Ella Fitzgerald's impact extends beyond her own performances to the untold stories of mentorship that shaped the careers of emerging talents. Dizzy Gillespie, Sarah Vaughan, and others found in Ella not just a musical collaborator but a guiding force that nurtured their artistic growth. The legacy of mentorship becomes a harmonious refrain in Ella's journey—a testament to her generosity and the symbiotic relationship between mentor and mentee. The untold anecdotes from jam sessions, backstage conversations, and collaborative efforts underscore Ella's role as a guardian of jazz tradition and an advocate for the next generation of musicians. The untold series delves into Ella's health struggles, a chapter often overshadowed by the brilliance of her musical triumphs. Vocal nodules and other health issues in the late

1950s posed significant challenges to her career. The untold narrative reveals Ella's determination to overcome health obstacles. The meticulous care she took to preserve her voice, the collaboration with medical professionals, and the resilience displayed in her return to the stage showcase an artist committed to her craft. The untold triumphs over health challenges become a chapter in Ella's life where the melody of resilience harmonizes with the discordant notes of physical struggle. The untold series concludes with reflections on Ella Fitzgerald's final years and the legacy she left behind. As health challenges mounted, Ella continued to perform, with her final public concert in 1991. The untold narrative reveals the emotional resonance of those performances—the bittersweet melody of a career approaching its final note. Ella's passing in 1996 marked the end of an era, but the echoes of her song continued to reverberate. The untold stories of her final years unveil the dichotomy of an artist determined to share her gift with the world while confronting the inevitability of time. The untold legacy of Ella Fitzgerald becomes an eternal echo—a melody that transcends time and resonates with new audiences, ensuring that the "First Lady of Song" remains an immortal presence in the symphony of American music. The posthumous tributes, the enduring celebrations of Ella's centennials, and the perpetual influence she exerts on the world of music all contribute to a legacy that refuses to fade. As the final note of the untold series resounds, we find ourselves immersed in the ever-expanding legacy of Ella Fitzgerald. It is a legacy that extends beyond the boundaries of jazz and popular music, reaching into the realms of activism, mentorship, and personal resilience. The symphony of Ella's life, when unveiled through the untold series, becomes a timeless composition—one that continues to captivate, inspire, and resonate with audiences around the world.

Printed in Great Britain
by Amazon